D0477794

HEROES AND WARRI

Richard Lionheart

THE CRUSADER KING

JOHN MATTHEWS
Plates by JAMES FIELD

Firebird Books

For all the Sons of Chivalry

Acknowledgements

My greatest debt, as always, is to my wife Caitlín, who typed most of the manuscript and supplied me with detailed information on aspects of twelfth century Europe. Additionally, in a work of this kind, acknowledgement must be made to the scholars and professional historians who charted the path, and without whose expertise, the author would have been hopelessly at sea. Thanks are also due to the French and Cyprus Tourist offices for permission to reproduce photographs.

J.M.

First published in the UK 1988 by Firebird Books
P.O. Box 327, Poole, Dorset BH15 2RG

Copyright © 1988 Firebird Books Ltd
Text copyright © 1988 John Matthews

Distributed in the United States by
Sterling Publishing Co, Inc,
2 Park Avenue, New York, NY 10016

Distributed in Australia by
Capricorn Link (Australia) Pty Ltd
PO Box 665, Lane Cove, NSW 2066

British Library Cataloguing in Publication Data

Matthews, John, *1948-*
    Richard Lionheart: the crusader king. —— (Heroes and warriors).
    1. Great Britain —— Kings and rulers ——
Biography
    I. Title II. Field, James III. Series
    942.03′2′0924   DA207

    ISBN 1 85314 007 4

All rights reserved. No part of this book may be reproduced or transmitted in any form or by any means, electronic or mechanical, including photocopying, recording or any informtion storage and retrieval system, without permission in writing from the Publisher.

Series editor Stuart Booth
Designed by Kathryn S.A. Booth
Typeset by Inforum Limited, Portsmouth
Colour separations by Kingfisher Facsimile
Colour printed by Riverside Printing Co (Reading) Ltd
Printed and bound in Great Britain at The Bath Press

Richard Lionheart
THE CRUSADER KING

Nottingham •

ENGLAND

• Oxford

London •

Winchester •

Canterbury •

BRABANT

FLANDERS

HAINAULT

CHAMPAGNE

NORMANDY

BLOIS

BRITTANY

MAINE

ANJOU

BURGUNDY

POITOU

TOURAINE

BERRI

LA MARCHE

ANGOUMOIS

PERIGORD

LIMOUSIN

AUVERGNE

PROVENCE

AGENAIS

TOULOUSE

GASCONY

NAVARRE

HOLY ROMAN EMPIRE

•••••••••••• Furthest extent of Richards lands

I knew the man, my dear master and a great king, who brought the leopards into the shield of England . . . Of him therefore . . . the hymned and reviled, the loved and loathed, spendthrift and miser, king and beggar . . . of King Richard Yea-and-Nay, so made, so called, I thus prepare my account.

(*The Life and Death of Richard Yea-and-Nay* Maurice Hewlett)

The Young Lion

The image that most people have of Richard I *Coeur de Lion* is of a brave, chivalrous knight and a fearless soldier. At times he attains almost mythical stature, appearing in the ballad cycles of Robin Hood as a noble saviour contrasted to bad King John.

The reality is somewhat different. Richard certainly was brave, and undoubtedly he was a good soldier. But he was also boorish, sadistic and greedy, once personally overseeing the execution of 2,500 Moslem prisoners. He preferred the furtherance of his own prestige over the needs of his kingdom – especially England, from where he was absent for almost the entire period of his kingship.

Historians are divided over Richard's abilities as a king. To some he was wholly bad, to others merely indifferent. Few find him more than adequate and even fewer describe him as good or even satisfactory. He knew no English and took no interest in what he must have regarded as a farflung outpost of his Angevin Empire – except for the revenues it could bring. Thus, the nineteenth century historian Bishop Stubbs said that Richard 'Was a bad king . . . his ambition that of a mere warrior. He would fight for anything whatever, but he would sell everything that was worth fighting for.'

Born on 8th September 1157 at Oxford, Richard's early days were totally overshadowed by his remarkable parents. King Henry II was wily, ambitious, and possessed of one of the keenest minds in Christendom. His mother, Eleanor of Aquitaine, was beautiful, vengeful and intellectually the equal of any man. They are two of the most colourful and exciting figures in the whole of medieval history. Being their son must have meant living constantly in the shadow of two brilliant luminaries. Henry was an exacting master, possessed of so much energy that it was popularly rumoured that he could fly, so swiftly did he travel from place to place. Eleanor became the centre of the world of troubadour song and romance, the world of knights and ladies, of adventure, love and the wanderings of brave men in search of noble deeds. Small wonder if their son grew up with a taste for chivalrous pursuits, warlike deeds and sometimes foolhardy enterprise.

5

Unlike his father, Richard was no statesman. His ability to upset people and drive wedges between himself and those who were supposed to be his allies was famous. One such affront, to the Archduke of Austria, later cost him his freedom and caused him to suffer a long imprisonment from which he was only freed at huge expense – much of which was raised by his neglected kingdom of England.

A Family of Conflict

Richard was brought up in France at his mother's court at Poitou. Eleanor and Henry had separated unofficially and there was no love lost between them. Richard was parcelled out to his mother, just as their other sons, Henry, Geoffrey and John, were kept by their father. Perhaps Richard had the best of it: at Queen Eleanor's court he encountered troubadours and intellectuals who taught him the social graces. In addition, he was able to take part in furious knockabout tournaments (Henry had banned them in England, deeming them a threat to public order) and this early training stood Richard in good stead in later life.

Certainly, there was nothing peaceful in the relationships between either the brothers or their father. In a chamber of the palace of Winchester, a fresco depicted an eagle being attacked by its fledglings. This was designed by Henry II himself in token of the way in which his own offspring spent most of their lives fighting against him. A strong man himself, Henry bred strong sons for whom even the great Angevin Empire was too small. For years the family spent most of their time in internecine struggle.

The reasons for this constant conflict are not hard to fathom. In 1170, Henry's eldest son was crowned by the Archbishop of York and was henceforward called 'the Young King' Henry. Richard, as second son, had been promised Aquitaine by his mother and had done homage to Louis VII of France. Geoffrey, the third son, was to marry the heiress to the Dukedom of Brittany. Between them the three sons held title to most of Henry II's kingdom – but title only. Henry II was barely thirty years of age and in the prime of his life. It would be a long time before anyone inherited – and his sons knew that sooner or later Henry would take something from them to give to the youngest of them all, John.

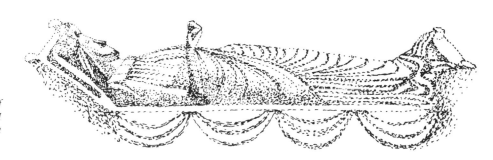

Tomb effigies of Eleanor of Aquitaine and of Henry II (opposite) from Fontrevault Abbey.

The upshot was that Richard, Geoffrey and the Young King Henry went to the court of the French King. From there they began formulating plans to take what they saw as rightly theirs, without waiting for their father's demise. Eleanor, disguising herself as a man, attempted to join them, but was captured and spent the rest of Henry II's reign in prison.

It was a strange situation, which must have made a lasting impression on Richard, who was more than usually close to his mother. Perhaps because of this he contrived to fight on even after his brothers had surrendered to the Old King. Finally, he too was forced to submit by Henry's superior forces and greater supply of money. Rather than punish him for the attempted rebellion, Henry gave Richard the task of quelling the very Aquitainian rebels from whom he had so recently looked for support.

It is typical of Richard that he accepted the task with alacrity and succeeded with such brilliance that almost overnight he became recognized as a famous warrior.

This did not please his elder brother, the Young King, who demanded that both Richard and Geoffrey should swear formal allegiance to him. This Henry almost persuaded them to do – until the Young King also demanded that Richard should swear his oath on a holy relic; at which Richard simply turned round and declared that Aquitaine was his anyway by right from his mother and had nothing to do with anyone else.

This so angered Henry II that he ordered his other sons to curb Richard's pride. Then, when both sides began to raise armies, he attempted to call a halt before civil war divided the Angevin Empire in half. In the end, by a touch of irony, the older Henry fought side by side with Richard against the other two brothers, thus reversing the roles of the earlier rebellion and causing the new French King, Philip II, to await the outcome with interest.

Then everything changed. In June 1183, the Young King fell victim to a sudden attack of dysentery and died a few days later. Richard was now heir to the throne of the Angevin Empire.

Henry II now hoped that things would settle down, and suggested that Richard should hand over Aquitaine to John, the youngest son. This

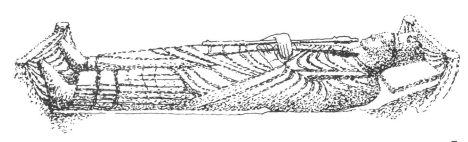

Richard refused to do, and once again the family brawls began. They might have continued unabated until Henry II's death, but two important factors altered the stakes for all the players in this complex game of dynastic skulduggery. First, only three years after the death of the Young King, Geoffrey, heir to Brittany, died in a tournament, leaving Richard and John as the only brothers to continue the struggle. The second factor was the appearance on the scene of a common enemy – though not immediately recognized as such. This was Philip II of France, whose extravagant plans for the future of his kingdom included the destruction of the Angevin Empire. Wooing first John and then Richard, Philip succeeded in keeping them at each other's throats, or at Henry's coat-tails, for several more years. Then, in 1187 an event occurred which was to change not only Richard's life, but the history of Europe and much of the rest of the world for generations to come.

Epoch of Change – Twelfth Century Europe

The twelfth century was an extraordinary period in many ways. It saw the laying to rest of the old war-torn, Dark-age Europe and the emergence of a distinct and purposeful civilization, which we now recognize as the first flowering of the Middle Ages. With the establishment of strong dynasties, civil wars and baronial insurrections were quelled or kept under control. European population began to expand in the more settled times. It was the time for the dissemination and transcription of stories and songs by means of travelling storytellers and poets; many of these, like Chrétien de Troyes and certain trouvères and troubadours received royal patronage. Stories of the great heroic kings like Arthur and Charlemagne were on everyone's tongue.

Crusades against Islam

Medieval North European civilization was to some extent an insular entity, shielded from its own past and from an encroaching future. Christianity had formalized society, bringing a standardization to culture, learning and administration. The Christianization of the rest of Europe and Russia was steadily progressing, though the fragmentation of the Christian church into Catholic West and Orthodox East was of recent origin: one clause of the creed – that the Holy Spirit proceeded from the Father 'and from the Son' (*filioque*) – had caused the Pope of Rome and the Patriarch of Byzantium to bombard each other with bulls and writs of excommunication. The West upheld the *filioque* clause; the East did not. And so the mutual help and support which should have

The Second Great Seal of Richard I, which shows him seated between the Moon and the Sun and bearing the symbols of his sovereignty.

8

typified Christian brothers became a stick which the Western church used in the coming crusade to beat Orthodox and infidel alike.

The idea of holy war (*jihad*) was native to Islam, a method of Moslem expansionism, but it was in Spain that Christianity first borrowed this notion. Roland's stand at Roncevalles against the Moslem army and El Cid's long campaign against the Moorish occupation of Spain vaunted the virtuous defence of Christendom. The feats of both heroes were the stuff of epic song. And so, when Byzantian emperor Alexius I appealed to Pope Urban II for help against the Seljuk Turks in Asia Minor, Urban saw the chance to vindicate the Western Church and show himself magnanimous to his Orthodox brothers. He sent the call through Europe to mobilize all Christian kings to liberate Jerusalem and the Holy Sepulchre. Jerusalem had been in Arab hands since the seventh century and the Holy Sepulchre was empty, but such was the emotional fervour stirred up by Urban's preachers that the First Crusade was launched and a new kind of 'holy war' was under way.

The old dictum 'might is right' which had typified the early years of the second millennium, was transformed to 'might *for* right'. Instead of fighting each other and laying waste Europe, crusading-spirited warriors now had licence to fight Moslems and plunder the infidels' land. The times were such that Christianity, whose founder taught brotherly love and forebearance, was quite incapable of applying these precepts within its own jurisdiction. The lesser evil was to syphon off the unschooled violence which was wrecking Europe and to apply it usefully elsewhere. It was in this early training ground that Britain discovered its propensity for colonization and love of Empire.

Despite their natural animosity, Christians and Moslems learned much from each other. Among the most famous of these cultural exchanges was chess, which was introduced into Spain during the tenth century. This reproduction from a thirteenth century chess manual shows a Christian and a Moslem playing a game.

9

Slaying Orthodox Christians, Jews and Moslems with great impartiality on their way, it took the crusaders two years to reach Jerusalem. There, many promptly claimed lands and titles and chose to remain. These men appreciated the riches of Islamic culture and technical achievement – and, doubtless, enjoyed the heady freedom of land without feudal obligations entailed to some ruthless overlord. It was these men who formed their own alliances and accommodations with Moslem rulers in exchange for peace. In contrast, the military orders like the Knights Templar undertook serious duties in protecting poor pilgrims from marauding bands of Moslems, as well as acting as an independent body of warrior-monks. The pattern of Europe was squarely placed upon the city of Jerusalem when, in 1100, Baldwin of Boulogne became the first King of Jerusalem. This was a political expediency which, in the later Middle Ages, was to become an empty if honourable title borne by otherwise undistinguished European rulers.

The Second Crusade was a less spectacular affair, failing because of many factors: the North German princes decided to direct their crusade against the pagan, Slavonic-speaking Wends; the French forces nearly attacked Constantinople as a result of severe relations between East and West; the native crusader barons were more determined to sustain their alliances with Moslem rulers in the Middle East than to help the next wave of crusaders (who might themselves claim lands).

Angevin Squabbles

While the Second Crusade was dragging on, Richard's father Henry II was consolidating his dynastic empire and England was in a state of civil war – which explains why no English king had yet appeared personally in the crusades.

Henry I of England, William the Conqueror's son, had left only one heir, Matilda, whom he had married to Henry V of Germany, the Holy Roman Emperor. At his death, Matilda's claim was overlooked in favour of Henry I's nephew, Stephen. There had ensued a formidable civil war, with the barons backing one side and then the other, while the Angevins undermined Stephen's kingship with carefully laid plans of their own.

Matilda's German husband had died in 1126. Henry I, her father, had ordered her back home to be used as a dynastic pawn. He rapidly re-established his alliance with the Angevin heir, Geoffrey, Duke of Anjou and Maine, by marrying him to his daughter. Matilda was still only 25 and Geoffrey a mere 14, but it was the wisest thing Henry I did in order to secure his dynastic survival (after the disastrous loss of his heir when the White Ship sank with loss of all hands, leaving him only a single female heir).

Geoffrey supported his wife's cause with vigour, but with two sets of lands to administer, Geoffrey attended to the French territories while

Geoffrey Plantagenet, Count of Anjou, as depicted in his tomb effigy.

Matilda went to uphold her claims to the queenship of England. The early life of their son, Henry II, was marked by the wrangle between Stephen and Matilda for the sovereignty of England. His succession to the English crown in 1154 at the age of 21 was hailed with relief by those worn down by insurrection and counter-bargaining. Anarchy was over and there now began the reign of one of the strongest kings ever to rule England, one whose territories and titles gave him authority over a great part of north-western Europe. He was count of Anjou in Maine after the death of his father; he was Duke of Normandy by right of his mother and Duke of Aquitaine by right of his wife, Eleanor, the divorced wife of King Louis VII of France. The only part of France which the French kings could claim as independent territory was restricted to north-eastern France and what is now Belgium. Such was the extent of the Angevin Empire. After decades of civil strife, Henry II was able to strengthen England and leave a vast domain to his sons – as previously described. The extent of the territory to be administered and the fact that Henry and Eleanor had four strong sons to inherit these lands was to prove a problem. For though Henry I had left England in a very confused state because he had only a daughter to inherit his title, Henry II's problem was quite the reverse.

With England once more stabilized, it could now afford to look beyond its own divisions and take a role in the affairs of Europe. Henry's

Armour and weapons from the First Crusade were closer in style to those of the Norman Conquest. A comparison with later styles shows the way in which armour developed in the years separating the first and third ventures into the Holy Land.

life-long role had been the Kingship of England, it was for his sons to look abroad for glory in battle.

Crusader King

Ever since the end of the First Crusade in 1100 and the unsuccessful conclusion of the Second in 1184, the tiny Christian Kingdom of Jerusalem – Outremer or the Land Beyond the Sea – had maintained a slender toehold on the eastern seaboard of the Holy Land. Surrounded on every side by the followers of Mohammed – who also laid claim to Jerusalem and its lands – it was only a matter of time before war broke out in earnest.

Then news reached Europe in 1187 of a great battle fought at Hattin, close to the Sea of Galilee. Here the Christian army, lead by Guy of Lusignan, the King of Jerusalem, had been utterly overwhelmed by a Moslem army lead by Al-Malik al-Nasir Salah ed-Din Yusuf, better known as Saladin. Guy was himself captured, and every surviving member of the two great military orders of the Templars and Hospitallers were executed. Jerusalem, the very heart of Christendom, had been captured and it could only be a matter of time before the remaining Christian forces, still holding on at Tyre, Tripoli and Antioch, were overcome or expelled.

A cry for help went out to Kings and Princes of the West, and Richard was one of the first to respond, receiving in November 1187 the piece of material cut into the shape of a cross which was the badge of all crusaders.

He did so without waiting for his father's permission. It was not until the end of the same year that Henry and Philip of France followed suit. Neither really wanted to take the Cross, being more concerned with their own affairs and plots against each other. However, public opinion and a gathering tide of religious fervour forced them to join their brother monarchs in swearing to raise armies to recapture the Holy City.

The rewards offered to those who did so were not inconsiderable. There were plenary indulgences, which meant the immediate forgiveness of all past sins and the promise of a place in heaven if they fell in battle. Also, on a more mundane level, there was the postponement of any financial debts then owing until such time as they returned from the crusade. This lead to numerous less-than-chivalrous characters joining the Christian armies for their own reasons. Yet there was also a genuine upsurge of religious feeling, of anger and hatred towards the infidels who had dared seize back the 'holy earth' so dearly bought with the blood of the First Crusade.

Mail hauberk of the kind worn by the crusaders in Richard's time.

12

Nonetheless, that inspired teacher Bernard of Clairvaux, who later on founded the Cistercian Order, knew well the innermost hearts of the army when he preached a sermon containing what must surely be the earliest ever advertising campaign:

O mighty soldier, O man of war, you now have a cause for which you can fight without endangering your soul . . . Or are you a shrewd business man, a man quick to see the profits of this world? If you are, I can offer you a splendid bargain. Don't miss this opportunity. Take the sign of the Cross . . . It doesn't cost much to buy and if you wear it with humility you will find it is worth the Kingdom of Heaven!

Stirred by thoughts of heroic deeds against the cruel and monstrous Saracens, Richard chafed, waiting for his father and Philip of France to settle their differences. Meetings between the two monarchs were arranged, but rather than bringing peace to the two countries, fresh hostilities broke out. Richard, alarmed that his father would appoint his younger brother as heir, tried to force Henry's hand by allying himself with Philip. In 1189 they invaded Maine and Henry, his tireless energy at last exhausted, fell ill. He withdrew to his favourite castle at Chinon and there, on 6th July he died, having learned at the last that his favourite son John had joined the rebels against him.

Richard was now King by right of birth and seniority. He visited his father's body where it lay in the abbey church of Fontrevault. Showing no emotion, he remained only a few minutes before turning away. It is said that as he left, blood flowed from the nostrils of the dead king, a fact which some took as a sign since the body of a murdered man will bleed in the presence of his murderer; but Henry's death was the outcome of a life lived at full tilt. Richard's only part was to hasten his father more quickly towards his end.

Richard I was crowned in England at Westminster on 3rd September 1189 and immediately set about raising money for the crusade. He sold castles, manors, privileges, public offices, even towns. He is said to have remarked: 'I would sell London, if I could find anyone rich enough to buy it.'

Finally, he sailed from Dover on 11th December 1189. Before he departed, he did his best to curb Prince John's ambition by giving him several huge tracts of English land in Derbyshire, Somerset, Dorset, Devon and Cornwall. At the same time, John was made Earl of Gloucester, and awarded the lands of Mortain in Normandy – to which he was instantly banished for a term of three years, Richard's clearest vote of no confidence in his brother.

The plan was for Richard and Philip to meet at Vézelay on 1st April 1190 and then to leave together for the Holy Land. Then news came that Philip's wife, Queen Isabel, had died suddenly. A further delay ensued and it was not until July that the two great armies finally set forth on the third anniversary of the Battle of Hattin. When Richard finally took up the scrip and staff of a pilgrim, the latter broke under him. Undeterred by

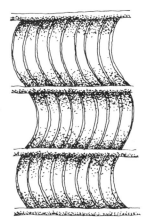

So-called 'banded mail' from which crusader armour was made. It could withstand all but point-blank arrows.

this ill omen, he set forth, intending to win not only fame and fortune but lands as well, which he had agreed to share equally with Philip. Their army has been estimated at between 6000 and 8000 men – a huge number for the time. It would be some four years before Richard saw England again. In the intervening time, he would become a changed man, as would many who set out with such high hopes to win back the holy earth of Outremer.

The Third Age

The helm of Richard Coeur de Lion.

The journey from Marseilles to the Holy Land should have taken fifteen days. It took Richard ten months; having set out filled with enthusiasm and burning ambition, the whole of the journey was fraught with disasters and setbacks.

At Lyons, the bridge over the Rhone collapsed from the weight of the men trying to cross – though fortunately only two were drowned. Richard had to organize a bridge of boats before he could cross. When he finally reached Marseilles, he expected to find the fleet of over a hundred ships which he had commissioned in advance. Instead, he found that they were still in Portugal, where their captains had become involved in the war against the Moors.

Furious, Richard hired thirty ships from the Marseilles merchants and set sail for Genoa, where Philip had arrived before him and promptly fallen ill. When the two kings met they had the first of many quarrels. Philip asked for the loan of five ships; Richard offered three. Philip refused and the stubborn men parted with harsh words.

Richard now pressed on to Salerno, where he wanted to discuss a recurrent ague with the city's famous doctors. There he learned that the original fleet was now in Sicily and he hastened on to Messina to join them.

He found Philip there before him and about to disembark. It seemed the two kings were trying to race each other to the Holy Land; certainly they wanted as little of each other's company as possible. Philip sailed but was forced to turn back almost at once by the weather. Once again, the two kings were stranded together at a time when the kingdom of Sicily was at a particularly explosive juncture in its long and turbulent history.

14

Embarkation for the crusade, from a fourteenth century miniature.

After the death of Sicily's most recent king, William II, a dispute arose over the succession, which should have gone to William's aunt; she was related to the son of the German Emperor, Frederick Barbarossa. This so alarmed the Sicilians, who wanted nothing to do with a German prince, that they gave the throne to William's illegitimate cousin, Tancred of Lecca, an ambitious man famed for his ugliness of both temper and physique.

The problem which arose when Richard's army arrived was caused by Tancred's withholding of a dowry promised to Richard's sister Joan – as well as the small matter of a legacy left by William II to Henry, who had been his father-in-law. Henry had died only a few weeks before William and this, so far as Tancred was concerned, meant that the arrangement was void. Of course, Richard disagreed and demanded payment in gold and ships for his army.

For a time, things hung in the balance, until Richard finally lost patience and took the city of Messina. This act was in opposition to Philip, who when the city had fallen, demanded that his own flag be raised over it, thus adding his own stake to any claim made upon Tancred.

Reluctantly, the Sicilian monarch paid up 20,000 ounces of gold for the unpaid dowry, and a further 20,000 ounces when Richard arranged a marriage between one of Tancred's daughters and his nephew and heir, Arthur of Brittany. In return, Richard promised military aid, if it should be needed, against the new German emperor. (Frederick Barbarossa had been drowned while his own crusading venture had barely started.)

By this time it was towards the end of October 1190 and too late to make the sea crossing to the Holy Land. Richard and Philip decided to

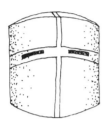

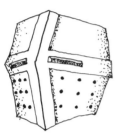

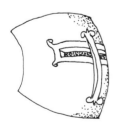

Helmets of the kind worn by the men who marched to the Holy Land with Richard.

winter in Sicily, and there celebrated Christmas in style, while the Christian forces across the sea suffered terrible privations from disease and starvation.

Also, while he was in Sicily, Richard heard that the current abbot of the monastery of Calabria, Joachim of Fiore, had announced a unique system of prophetic insight based upon Biblical references. According to this divination, there were three ages of mankind, the third of which – the Age of the Spirit – was about to dawn. This would be signified by the defeat of Saladin, whom Joachim saw as the current Antichrist.

Richard at once demanded to know when this would happen and was told 1194 (four years hence). 'Then,' said Richard, 'I have gone on crusade too soon.'

Joachim reassured him that he was needed and would have God on his side. Richard had to be satisfied with this response, but he was clearly convinced thereafter that he was destined to overcome Saladin.

Mediterranean Marriage

February of 1191 came and still Richard delayed. A fresh quarrel broke out between him and the King of France. Richard had been engaged to Philip's sister Alys since 1169. Suddenly, Eleanor of Aquitaine, seventy years old but as active as ever, arrived in Messina with a new bride for her son. Berengaria was the daughter of the King of Navarre and a good match for Richard – but Philip, needless to say, was furious. The argument raged for days, then Richard suddenly declared that he would not marry Alys because she had been his father's mistress and had borne him a son. This may or may not have been true, though knowing Henry II, it may well have been. Nevertheless, Richard declared that he had witnesses to prove it and Philip made a tactful withdrawal, secretly plotting with Tancred.

Richard, however, had already made overtures of friendship to the Sicilian king and cemented this by giving him a rich and generous gift – Excalibur, the magical sword of King Arthur. (Quite how he had come by this weapon, since it was cast into the lake at the conclusion of that great king's reign, is not recorded!)

By then, it was the season of Lent. Since he could not get married (marriages were never solemnized during Lent) Richard decided to delay no longer, Philip having sailed already. Also, Richard thought to have the marriage ceremony performed in the Holy Land. Thus, on 10th April 1191, he finally sailed from Sicily. His fleet is said to have numbered more than 200 vessels and his army had grown even larger since leaving France.

But he was still fated not to complete his voyage without problems. A storm blew up before they were three days out from Sicily, and several ships were either wrecked or blown off course. Among the latter was the ship carrying Berengaria and Richard's sister Joan.

Richard leads a relief force to the aid of the beleaguered city of Acre. He is the first to leap ashore, to the delight and relief of the garrison commander.

Reaching the island of Rhodes, Richard decided to wait there while he sent fast ships in pursuit of the missing vessel. He soon learned that it had come ashore on the island of Cyprus, where the ruler, Isaac Ducas Comnenus, had already seized several survivors from other wrecks and now virtually held Richard's bride and his sister to ransom.

At once, Richard set forth for Cyprus and after unsuccessful negotiations with Isaac, laid siege to Limassol. He captured this easily and chased Isaac inland, having ensured the safety of Berengaria and Joan. At this juncture he received a visit from the leaders of the Christian forces in the Holy Land, who came to ask for his support against Philip of France. That wily monarch had reached Acre in April and at once began plotting to make himself King of Outremer, pushing the incumbent Guy of Lusignan off the throne.

Richard at once agreed to help in return for assistance in his immediate design, the conquest of Cyprus. He received the help he needed and in the next three months showed his superb generalship by totally subduing the island. He captured Isaac's wife and daughter, and having promised not to put the former ruler in irons, had silver chains made for him.

Richard now married Berengaria in a wedding long remembered for its splendour. He seems to have been content with his wife, though he saw little enough of her in the years which followed.

Kolossi Castle near Limassol, Cyprus. Richard landed here in 1191 in pursuit of his bride Berengaria. He conquered Cyprus in three months and established there a base of operations for the Christian forces in the East.

Richard was a powerful and ruthless adversary, earning his title 'Lionheart' from the Saracens who were his bitterest foes. In a pitched battle, the armour and weaponry of the Christian army proved superior.

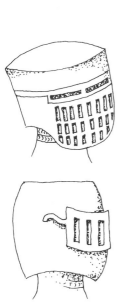

The Christian base on Cyprus was of immense strategic importance for the crusaders, who now had both a jumping-off point for their armies and a supply base which was virtually impregnable.

On 5th June, Richard finally set sail on the final leg of his long journey, reaching Tyre next day. Here the garrison, acting on advice from Philip, refused to admit him. Enraged, Richard sailed on and landed at Acre, joining the besieging army on 8th June.

For Richard, the Third Age foretold by Joachim of Fiore had now begun.

Weapons and Warfare

The period between the end of the twelfth century and the middle of the thirteenth saw several crucial innovations in weaponry and armour which helped make the medieval knight what he was always intended to be: a superb fighting machine.

Within a space of some twenty years, chain mail virtually replaced a variety of earlier forms of armour. Additionally, the development of the huge 'pot' helm, which enclosed all of the head rather than just the skull, made its wearer virtually invulnerable against anything less than a blow delivered with the full weight of a sword or axe.

We take chain mail very much for granted, seeing it depicted in paintings of the time, or in recent cinematic extravaganzas. Yet it was by no means easy to manufacture. We tend to forget the immense labour involved in forging the literally thousands of wire rings, which had then to be beaten flat, holes drilled into each end, and rivets added. For additional strength, mail coats were constructed from patches of four links to one. They were then further riveted, welded, or soldered and various parts strengthened even further by doubling or even trebling the rings.

Providing it was kept free from rust, a good coat of mail, made by a master armourer, would last its owner a lifetime. It was kept clean by the simple method of scrubbing it with fine sand – a commodity in no short supply during Richard's desert campaigns!

The helm evolved gradually from the conical Norman helmet, ear flaps being added. These flaps gradually grew larger until they met the nasal and became a single sheet of metal, with slits to allow vision and holes for breathing. These massive objects sometimes weighed several pounds, and with the addition of padding must have been unbearably hot. If we imagine the knight of Richard's time riding into battle with a padded gambeson (quilted body-armour), chain mail shirt and hose, topped by the huge helm, and swinging a heavy longsword – all in the blistering heat of the desert and against a much lighter-clad adversary –

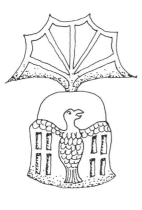

Further examples of crusader helmets

18

we may wonder that the crusaders managed to win *any* battles. But these were superb fighting men, forged by the iron wills and driving energy of their leaders until they could master any terrain or circumstance.

Origins of Heraldry

With the development of the all-enclosing helm came a further necessity – that of recognition. It is generally accepted that during the period of the First Crusade knights began to wear distinguishing marks of one kind or another. Such marks were either on their shields, or in the form of an effigy attached to the top of the helm. Thus Richard himself is depicted on his Great Seal with a lion *passant* on the side of his helm, topped by a fan-shaped ornament.

A Spanish poet of the eleventh century describes how:

> *Some of the knights placed upon their armour*
> *signs that were different one from another*
> *in order to be known thereby, while others*
> *placed them upon their heads, or on their horses.*
> *(Lays de Partida)*

These distinguishing devices developed in time into the system we now know as heraldry.

Arms and Weaponry

The sword and mace were still favourite weapons for hand-to-hand fighting, though the famous charge of the Frankish knights with levelled lances was still an awesome and terrible thing to the lightly-armed Saracens.

Swords were about thirty inches in length, the blade two-edged and tapering towards a diamond-shaped point. The quillons were short at this time, curving slightly towards the blade, while the grip was short without a swell, the pommel being usually a simple knob or wheel-shape.

Richard is said to have favoured the axe as a hand-to hand weapon, and a contemporary poem records that he had one made specially before departing for the Holy Land:

> *Then King Richard I understond,*
> *Ere he went out of Engilond,*
> *Let make an axe for the nones*
> *Therewith to cleve the Saracens' bones.*
> *The head in sooth was wrought full weele,*
> *Thereon was twenty pounds of steele,*
> *And when he came to Cyprus londe*
> *This iron axe he took in honde.*

Against this armoured might the Saracens had little or no defence save superior numbers and the horrors of heat and sickness. Their armour,

Knight in crusader style of mailed hauberk and surcoat with helmet, shield and sword: from the effigy on the tomb of Lord Robert of Tattershall at Kirkstead in Lancashire.

An axe-head from the period of the second Crusade.

though skilfully made and often beautiful, was far less durable than that of the crusaders. They had always relied on speed and skill in horsemanship, which enabled them to dash in upon their adversaries, fire off a salvo from their short but deadly bows, and then retreat before any reprisal.

But Saracen arrows did not have the power of penetration necessary to pierce the heavy mail hauberks of the Christian knights, and whenever their numbers were inferior they were frequently overwhelmed by the sheer weight and ferocity of their opponents.

Cavalry Tactics

The great hero Rodrigo del Bivar – El Cid – had been the first person to use the weight of heavily armed cavalry against the more lightly clad Moors. Richard and the Crusaders adopted this method of battle, countering the Saracens' horsemanship and displaying great military skill against the Turkish cavalry of Saladin. In a sense, Richard consolidated the supremacy of the Christian cavalry which El Cid had established over Islam in Spain and he proved this to great effect in the running battles which followed the siege of Acre.

Two knights in quilted armour of the type called gambeson. Though beginning to go out of fashion in Richard's time, many of his soldiers would still have worn it.

The Kingdom of Christ

The siege of Acre began in 1189, when Guy of Lusignan, desperate to renew his failing fortunes, had marched with a suicidally-small force against the greatest city in the Holy Land. Despite lack of strength, his forces had held on grimly; gradually reinforcements had filtered through until they were sufficient to establish a blockade on the landward side of the city.

At that point, a stalemate resulted, with the Christian forces in turn surrounded by Saladin, and enough Saracen ships getting through to keep the besieged forces at Acre sufficiently provisioned. Philip's arrival, shortly before, had considerably boosted the morale of the besiegers. However, Guy of Lusignan was far from pleased since Philip at once began plotting to make himself King of Jerusalem. Added to this, Guy had another adversary in the shape of Conrad of Montferrat, who had won an overwhelming victory against Saladin by repulsing the Moslem attack on Tyre. Thus Conrad's star was in the ascendant, while Guy's fell. It was this situation which had prompted Lusignan to lay siege to Acre and to invite Richard's support.

The arrival of the English King further heartened the attacking force. Not only did Richard bring with him a large army, he also had a number of siege engines with which he began systematically to batter at the walls of Acre.

20

Nevertheless, the state of siege continued for a further month. Both Richard and Philip sickened with what appears to have been a form of scurvy; and for a while Richard's life was threatened. But he was soon well enough to be carried in a litter to within the sight of the battered walls and to offer a gold piece to any man who could bring him a stone from those walls.

The continuing pressure began to tell on the grim defenders of the city. Whenever a section of the walls collapsed – either from the battery of the siege engines or from miners working beneath them – the Christian forces attacked. Upon each attack, the defenders sounded their drums, and Saladin at once attacked the Christian camp from behind.

Nevertheless, the outcome was inevitable and on 12th July 1189, the beleaguered garrison capitulated, agreeing terms of surrender which included a large ransom, the release of 1,500 prisoners held by Saladin, and the restoration of the True Cross, which had been captured during the fall of Jerusalem.

There then occurred one of those events which, though seemingly of minor effect, was to have far-reaching repercussions.

As the triumphant Christian forces entered Acre, the Kings of England and France both set up their standards, thereby claiming not only the victory but also a part of the spoils. Alongside their flags was that of another crusader lord, Duke Leopold of Austria; he had nominal command over the remnant of Emperor Frederick Barbarossa's army, which had continued to Acre after Barbarossa's death. However, despite his honorary title, Leopold had no money to buy his supporters. In contrast, Richard and Philip were trying to outbid each other by offering first three and then four gold pieces to any soldier who took service with them.

This placed Leopold in a very subordinate position, and the act of raising his standard and claiming a share in the booty of the fallen city was a foolish one, to say the least. In fact, his banner flew beside those of England and France for a few hours only. Then it was unceremoniously pulled down and trodden into the mud by English soldiers, who must have been acting with Richard's approval at the very least.

Naturally, Leopold protested, but he was virtually brushed aside. He left the camp a few days later and returned to Austria, but he was not to forget the slight done to him by the English king. Soon, the day was to come when Richard had grave cause to regret his actions and the humiliation of Leopold.

With Acre in the hands of the Christians, Philip now declared his intention of returning to France. Despite every effort of his followers to prevent it, he gave half his share of booty to Conrad of Montferrat. Then, leaving half his army under the command of the Duke of Burgundy, he set sail for home.

Richard was far from happy at this turn of events. He was suspicious of Philip's intentions and extracted a promise from him that the French

During the Siege of Acre, Richard offered a gold piece to any man who would bring him back a stone from the walls of the city.

King would not attack Angevin lands while he, Richard, remained on the crusade. Then he set about concluding the terms of surrender negotiated with the Moslem garrison of Acre, which involved a large-scale exchange of prisoners. For whatever reason – though possibly a simple one of logistics – Saladin was not able to meet the deadline. Richard therefore had 2,500 prisoners taken outside the walls and executed in sight of Saladin's army. It was an act of barbarism for which there is no reasonable excuse. Richard himself looked on as his soldiers, remembering perhaps their own fallen comrades, fell upon the bound prisoners and literally hacked them to pieces.

Two days later, he marched out of Acre on the next leg of his campaign to win back 'God's Kingdom'. With Philip gone, he was now the senior commander of the crusade. He paid the remnant of the French army from his own coffers in order to prevent them from reducing the

Richard watches coldly as 2,500 Saracen prisoners are executed in front of their comrades after the Battle of Acre.

THE SIEGE OF ACRE 1189-91 and RICHARD'S ROAD TO JERUSALEM 1191-2

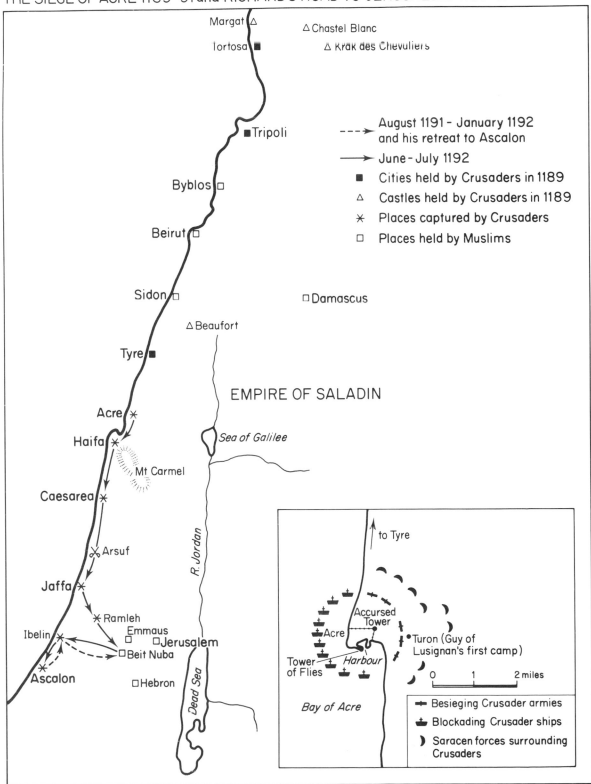

Margat △

△ Chastel Blanc

■ Tortosa

△ Krak des Chevaliers

■ Tripoli

– – – → August 1191 – January 1192
and his retreat to Ascalon

——→ June – July 1192

■ Cities held by Crusaders in 1189

△ Castles held by Crusaders in 1189

✳ Places captured by Crusaders

□ Places held by Muslims

Byblos □

Beirut □

Sidon □

□ Damascus

△ Beaufort

Tyre ■

EMPIRE OF SALADIN

Acre ✳

Haifa ✳

Sea of Galilee

Mt Carmel

Caesarea ✳

Arsuf ✳

R. Jordan

Jaffa ✳

✳ Ramleh

Emmaus

Ibelin ✳

□ □ Jerusalem

□ Beit Nuba

Ascalon ✳

□ Hebron

Dead Sea

to Tyre

Accursed Tower

Acre

Turon (Guy of Lusignan's first camp)

Tower of Flies

Harbour

0   1   2 miles

Bay of Acre

⊢—⊣ Besieging Crusader armies

⚓ Blockading Crusader ships

❱ Saracen forces surrounding Crusaders

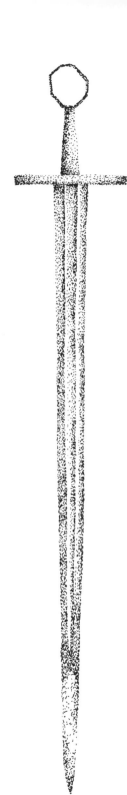

A crusader sword, typical of the type carried by Richard's army

Christian forces by their departure, and set forth to deal with Saladin.

It has been remarked by more than one historian that, whatever one's bias, the Saracen leader was altogether a more sympathetic character than Richard. Descended from a family of Kurdish army officers, Saladin had become Vizier of Egypt in 1169; and when the ruler of Syria, Nur-el-Din, died in 1174, Saladin married his widow and rapidly established himself as a new champion of the Moslem world. Convinced that it was his destiny to drive the Christians out of the Holy Land, he took up a moral stance as well as a military one. Perhaps because of this, he is remembered as one of the most principled men of his time.

Generous even to his enemies, there is a consistent group of legends which suggest that he made several attempts to seek Richard's friendship. Indeed, there does seem to have existed a grudging respect between the two men who held the reins of power in the Holy Land for the next few years.

Running Battles

Once out of the protection afforded by the walls of Acre, Richard again showed his military genius by the tactics he adopted to deal with Saladin's famous Turkish cavalry.

Richard gave orders that the army should ride in close formation, keeping close to the sea, which thus protected their right flank; the infantry had the task of marching between their left flank and Saladin's force, which kept pace with him and sent in waves of skirmishes to worry him.

This continued all the way to Haifa and beyond. The crusaders suffered terribly from sunstroke, dysentery and the incessant Saracen attack. Yet they kept moving, slowly but surely, provisioned by the fleet which kept pace with them. After several weeks, Saladin at last realized that he must draw Richard into a direct confrontation; only thus would matters be decided.

The Battle of Arsuf took place on 7th October 1195 and lasted for most of the day. Throughout the morning, Richard held in check his strongest force – the mounted knights – and let the infantry take the brunt of the furious Saracen attack. He was waiting for the enemy to be fully engaged and for their mounts to grow tired. Nevertheless, the day was almost lost when the Hospitallers, who had taken a terrible beating, broke and charged. They could have carried the whole Christian army with them and thus opened its ranks to the swiftly weaving attack of the Saracen cavalry. But Richard personally rallied his forces, before they could become demoralized, and lead a tremendous onslaught with all the weight of his knights. They bore all before them. Saladin's hitherto invincible army was cut to ribbons.

A contemporary account says of Richard:

24

There the King, the fierce, the extraordinary King, cut down the Turks in every direction, and none could escape the force of his army, for wherever he turned, brandishing his sword, he carved a wide path for himself, cutting them down like a reaper with his sickle.

(trans: J. Gillingham.)

Combat between crusaders and Saracens during the period of Richard's activity in the Holy Land.

Three days later, the crusaders reached Jaffa, thus securing the port nearest to Jerusalem. The fleet dropped anchor and began to replenish the exhausted army, while Richard concentrated on constructing temporary walls, Saladin having providently dismantled them before withdrawing some months before.

Indecision and Anticlimax

Richard now had a difficult choice before him. He could advance inland towards Jerusalem, but this would risk his supply lines, which would be thinly stretched between the sea and the army. Alternatively he could continue along the coast to the port of Ascalon, which had greater strategic importance as the base for the Saracen fleet.

For a time, he did neither. Instead, he remained in Jaffa, strengthening its walls and refortifying castles along the road from Acre which Saladin had destroyed. He re-opened negotiations with the Saracen lord, making what now seems the frivolous offer that his sister Joan should marry Saladin's brother and that her dowry should include the coastal towns from Ascalon to Acre. Needless to say, this idea failed to come to anything – though Saladin first of all gave his consent, presumably tongue in cheek, only to be told by Richard that Joan had flatly refused to marry an infidel.

Talks continued throughout the following year. So, too, did the steady, almost secret crusader advance. By December 1191 they were within twelve miles of Jerusalem.

Then, at that point, they turned back. Richard was worried about the increasing pressure on his supply lines. He knew also that even if he succeeded in capturing the Holy City, most of his army would swiftly melt away, their commitment to the crusade satisfied by having set foot on the holy earth at the middle of Christendom.

The whole army was shocked and disheartened by the decision. To many Richard was the greatest general they had known. He had defeated the great Saladin and led them through impossible country to within sight of their goal.

Many wept openly, others cursed their leader; and when the army reached Jaffa, many kept on to Acre, leaving Richard with a much diminished force. Nonetheless, he marched on to Ascalon and took it easily, Saladin having withdrawn to Jerusalem to await an attack which never came.

Richard now controlled the whole of the coastline of Outremer from Acre to Ascalon and swiftly set about consolidating his victories, making the roads safe and rebuilding castles destroyed by the Saracens.

But all was not well in the rest of the country. Political squabbles had broken out again between the supporters of Guy of Lusignan and Conrad of Montferrat. Then, to add to Richard's problems, he received news that his brother John was creating trouble in England, while Philip began threatening the borders of Normandy. It was essential for Richard to return home in order to look after his own affairs. However, before he could do so he had to ensure that Outremer had a strong king – otherwise all that he had achieved would have been lost.

He called a council of crusader lords and asked them to vote for a king. They came down unanimously in favour of Conrad, and Richard had to acknowledge the sense of this: Conrad was the stronger man; Guy had lost the battle of Hattin.

Conrad's triumph was short-lived. A few days later, he was murdered by two of the dreaded order of Assassin, an outlawed Moslem sect who spread a reign of terror throughout the Holy Land.

Conrad's widow, Isabella, had shut herself up in the city of Tyre, acting on her husband's dying instructions not to give up the keys of the city to anyone but Richard. (This was meant to keep it out of French hands.)

Richard's cousin, Henry of Champagne, now appeared on the scene. Incredibly, he wooed and won Isabella and some months later became Lord of Outremer, with Richard's approval. But Henry never styled himself King, since he could not be crowned in Jerusalem.

These events contrived to keep Richard from departing as soon as he had planned. Again, he found himself with two clear choices. He could

A contemporary portrait of
Saladin, Richard's greatest
adversary during the crusade.
As well as being a great general, Saladin was a notable statesman and generous opponent.

return to Europe and put an end to the plotting of John and Philip, but face the possibility of losing all he had gained in Outremer. Equally he could remain in the Holy Land for a longer period and face the possibility of having no lands to which he could return. Added to this dilemma was the pressure from the other crusader lords for him to stay and, under a truly united force, storm Jerusalem at last.

So agonizing was the decision that Richard became ill. When he recovered, he had made up his mind – he would stay until Easter of the following year and he would lead the Christian attack on the Holy City.

Filled with jubilation, the army set forth again to march the long, hot miles back to Jerusalem. Their journey was almost uneventful; but when they once again came within a few miles of their objective, Richard called a halt. Nothing, he realized, had really changed. The same problems as before faced those who succeeded in capturing the city. Suddenly, he declared that he would go no further as leader of the Christian forces. He would accompany them as a pilgrim – or not at all.

Despairing, the army conferred, realized they could never go further without their great captain. Wearily they turned back and marched once again to Ascalon. Once there, Richard re-opened discussions with Saladin, who swiftly agreed to allow the Christian force to remain on the coast, providing they abandoned Ascalon. Richard refused, only to learn that Saladin had marched on Jaffa and laid siege to the Christians within. He turned at once to relieve Jaffa, but arrived to see Saladin's banners already fluttering above the walls.

The garrison were just departing, having laid down their weapons. They saw the relief ships and swiftly renewed the attack. Richard himself leapt into the sea and waded ashore at the head of his men.

Jaffa was soon in crusader hands again. Saladin made a somewhat half-hearted effort at a surprise attack. This was beaten off with resounding losses for the Saracens, and Saladin re-opened negotiations for peace.

This time, Richard gave in over the question of Ascalon, in return for which the Moslem leader gave pilgrims permission to enter Jerusalem in peace. Richard himself did not avail himself of this offer: he would enter Jerusalem as a conqueror or not at all.

A few weeks later he left the Holy Land. Had he remained until Easter of 1193, as he had originally intended, history might have been very different: Saladin died suddenly in March of that year, thus removing the only real obstacle between the crusaders and the Holy City.

However, Richard was no longer there as leader. His chance of regaining Christ's kingdom had gone forever – and meanwhile an old enemy waited to settle a score.

Capture and Ransom

It had taken Richard far longer to reach the Holy Land than most people of that time. His journey homewards was to be just as protracted and led to an enormous upheaval throughout the Western world.

A few days out from Acre, Richard's fleet was caught in a storm and his ship, the *Franche-Nef*, became separated from the main body of the fleet. Forced to sail on, Richard learned that his enemies were waiting to imprison him at Marseilles. So, after encountering some pirates, whom he first successfully defeated, he then employed them to carry him secretly to a destination on the northern coast of the Adriatic.

However, disaster struck again and the pirate ship was wrecked on lands belonging to the German Emperor Henry VI, who had no cause to love Richard after he had backed Tancred of Sicily against him.

Richard's adventures now assumed an almost legendary quality. He travelled in disguise through the lands of his enemy, was captured, and released again. Finally, he fell into the hands of Duke Leopold of Austria,

who had left the crusades ignominiously after his standard had been torn down by Richard's men and who had borne a grudge ever since.

By now it was the end of 1192; Richard had been 'missing, presumed drowned' for almost a year. All kinds of rumours were rife. In England, Henry Longchamps, who had been left in charge of the kingdom by Richard in his absence, had been virtually overthrown by Prince John who attempted to raise a rebellion with support from disaffected Welsh barons.

It is at this point that there first appears the story of Richard's jongleur, Blondel. Having heard a rumour of his master's capture, Blondel is said to have travelled throughout Europe singing a song he had composed with Richard. He sang until one day he heard a response from a barred window in the castle of Dürnstein.

Whether or not there is any truth in this story, we cannot know. Certainly, there is no hard evidence to support it though it remains one of history's more romantic and well known tales. Whether by this means,

The castle of Dürnstein in Lower Austria where Richard was held to ransom by Archduke Leopold, in retaliation for the insults done to him by Richard's men. Legend has it that Blondel sang beneath the windows and so discovered his imprisoned master.

29

or by more orthodox communications, it soon became known that Richard was a prisoner, and there at once began a race to see who could raise the largest ransom for him – his friends or his enemies.

Naturally, Philip of France desired to capture his old enemy and lay claim to his lands. Prince John was content to let his brother rot rather than give up the power he had begun to acquire. John had already done homage to Philip for Richard's lands, and had promised to marry Philip's sister Alys, whom Richard had earlier refused.

The ransom for the captive king was set at 20,000 marks, a huge sum by the standard of the time, and various other difficult provisos hedged him round.

Moved from castle to castle to forestall any attempt at rescue, Richard finally faced his enemies at Speyer, not far from Wurtzburg, on 21–22nd March 1193. He was accused of plotting the death of Conrad of Montferrat; of supporting Tancred's illegal regime; and of the insult to Leopold of Austria. So calm, dignified and eloquent was Richard in response, that the Emperor Henry was moved to offer the kiss of peace, while others among his accusers wept openly.

Even so, the ransom was now increased to 100,000 marks, with 70,000 as a downpayment, and a further promise to supply men and arms to the German Emperor for a reconquest of Sicily.

Hard upon the heels of this came news that Philip had openly declared war on the Angevins and had attacked Normandy with some success. In England, John was being kept in check by a few of Richard's loyal supporters, and efforts were under way to raise the huge ransom.

For months, the incessant bargaining continued and Richard was virtually an object for auction among the crowned heads of Europe. Yet he proved himself a better politician than many had supposed, making himself so useful to Henry VI that the two virtually became allies. At one time Richard was even offered the crown of Portugal, which would have extended his empire still further.

Then, fearful of Richard's imminent release, Philip and John jointly made an offer of 150,000 marks in order to buy him from the Germans. This was tempting and would have made Richard a prisoner of Philip. Fortunately, Richard had now made a sufficient number of friends at the German court to ensure that the offer was rejected. However, Henry did raise the ransom money to match the French offer, and also insisted that Richard do homage to him for England.

By this time, the Lionheart was desperate to be free and would probably have agreed to anything. He offered to pay 100,000 marks to Henry and 50,000 to Leopold. So on these terms he was finally set free in March of 1194. He had been a prisoner for two years and his freedom had cost more than three times his own yearly income. He had also lost part of his lands to Philip. But he cared nothing except that he was free.

Leopold of Austria, condemned by the Church for his part in impris-

oning a crusader, refused to pay back the ransom. Strangely, not long after, his foot was crushed by a fall from his horse and he died a few months later from gangrene.

The Chateau Gaillard built at Richard's behest between 1194 and 1196. Dramatically situated, it became central to the defensive network between Richard's lands and those of Philip II.

Europe's Champion

Once back in England, Richard set about putting right the wrongs perpetrated by his brother, who had fled to France, and then began finding methods of regaining the money he had lost in buying his release. He intended to cross the channel to Normandy at the first opportunity and win back the lands he had lost to Philip and John.

Ably assisted by his new chancellor, Archbishop Hubert Walter, Richard raised sufficient revenue from the hard-pressed tax-payers of England to raise an army. In May 1194, he entered Normandy to a rapturous welcome. John, suddenly deciding that his brother might win the game they had been playing for the past ten years, left Philip and threw himself on Richard's mercy. Richard forgave him magnanimously, but saw to it that John had no further chance of betrayal.

Richard proceeded to march rings round his old enemy of France, capturing a large amount of booty – and a part of the royal archive which

31

Richard mortally wounded in the shoulder by an arrow shot by Bertrand de Gourdon, at the siege of Castle Chalus in Limousin, 1199. This depiction is from the fifteenth century manuscript the Chronique de Normandie.

contained the names of those among Richard's supporters who had promised aid to Philip if the need arose.

Richard seemed absolutely unstoppable. He had signed treaties with the Count of Toulouse and the King of Navarre even while he was still in prison. Effectively, he had Philip cut off. Even Pope Innocent III threatened the French King for repudiating the daughter of King Cnut of Denmark, whom he had married in 1193.

But Philip still had a powerful army and had succeeded in capturing a sufficient number of castles along the border of Normandy to enable him to mount raids deep into Richard's territory.

The struggle dragged on into 1195, and despite a treaty signed in January of the following year, hostilities continued, and in 1198 matters had still not improved. Another treaty was finally negotiated in 1199 by a papal legate and the two Kings met briefly, though remaining only in view of each other on separate banks of the Seine. Part of the agreement included a marriage between Philip's son Louis and Richard's niece, Blanche of Castille. It was an agreement which seemed likely to provide a peace both lasting and satisfactory to both sides.

Then disaster struck, and in a few weeks Europe's strongest champion was dead. Richard had always been reckless, allowing himself to be

Some of Richard's soldiers are aggrieved by the proud claims of the Austrian Archduke Leopold, who raised his standard between those of England and France. They pull down the Austrian standard, trampling it in the mud.

distracted by minor concerns to which others could have attended. Typically, it was this carelessness which cost him his life. Word reached him that a peasant had found some treasure and taken it to his lord, Archard of Chalus, who intended to keep it for himself. Richard thought otherwise, and took a large force to besiege Chalus' small castle. Tradition has it that there were barely fifteen men inside, ill-armed and ill-prepared to withstand a siege. During the fighting Richard received a wound in the shoulder from a cross-bow bolt. The wound festered and the bolt proved difficult to remove. Gangrene entered the wound and Richard realized that he was facing death. He wrote to Eleanor of Aquitaine, incredibly still active at nearly eighty years of age, bequeathing his realm to John, along with three-quarters of his treasure. The rest was to be distributed among the poor.

This sudden act of charity was followed by another generous decision: the man who had wounded him was brought before Richard who forgave him and ordered him set free. Richard then received the last rites and died in the evening, aged forty-one.

The empire he had left behind was no less extensive than that of his father, but it was a great deal less secure. John had none of his family's abilities and is typically remembered by the nickname 'Lackland'. Only a few years after he became king, he was forced to sign Magna Carta, giving more power than ever before to the barons of the realm. The loss of the royal treasure in the Wash concluded a catalogue of disasters. Perhaps in the shadow of a legend, he could have done no better.

Lionheart – Legend and Legacy

Richard *Coeur de Lion*, the Lionheart of England, was dead. He had already become something of a legend, and despite all his shortcomings,

This portrait of Richard I is based on contemporary pictures. He was short, red-haired and of a fiery, sometimes, ill-natured, sometimes generous temper.

Returning home to England in disguise, Richard was recognized and attacked by soldiers of Archduke Leopold of Austria, who subsequently kept the Lionheart hostage.

it is in this light that he is remembered. Yet he failed in his greatest enterprise: the capture of the Holy City. Equally, he was a poor king and a hotheaded – if courageous – leader, who died carelessly and without leaving an heir to his great empire.

When Archbishop Walter visited Jerusalem in 1192, he met Saladin and the two men discussed Richard at length. The Saracen who had been Richard's greatest enemy, had this to say:

I have long since been aware that your king is a man of honour and very brave, but he is impudent, indeed absurdly so, in the way he plunges into the midst of danger and in his reckless indifference to his own safety . . . I would like to have wisdom and moderation rather than an excessive wildness.

(trans: J. Gillingham)

His words proved fatally apt, but the legend only continued to grow after Richard's death. He had first received the title Lionheart at the start of the Crusade, when someone compared Philip to a lamb and Richard to a lion, and seemed to become beset with mythical associations. He is said to have convened his commanders in Winchester at the Round Table, believed to have belonged to King Arthur, and to have possessed the magical sword Excalibur. Later legends and popular folklore describe his meeting with Robin Hood in Sherwood Forest, and commend him for his resistance to John Lackland's plots. Indeed, it is this almost Hollywood-like story which is most familiar to us.

Saladin receiving the Bishop of Salisbury and other Christian pilgrims, whom he treated with respect and eventually permitted to enter Jerusalem.

The statue of Richard which stands outside of the Houses of Parliament in London.

At his death, the troubador, Gaucelem Faidit mourned him as 'the courageous and powerful King of the English,' and men who had fought at his side praised his courage and leadership.

As John Gillingham, one of his most recent biographers observed, it is a mistake to judge Richard by modern standards. As a man of the twelfth century, he was neither better nor worse than many others. As a symbol of the burgeoning chivalric ideals of the time, he was bound to be enshrined as a hero of his age. It is best that as such we remember him, forgetting the darker side of his nature – the slaughter of 2,500 prisoners at Acre and the greed which undoubtedly motivated much of his life. Better indeed, to remember him as a warrior in the heroic mould; a man who, in the end, would not have disappointed his exacting father.

He was Europe's Lionheart, and as such he continues to inspire with an idea of nobility which he may never have known. As well as a warrior, he was also a poet and a troubador who wrote a number of songs which have survived. One of these, written while he was still in

35

prison, sums him up best and perhaps serves best as a reminder of his finer qualities:

> *Ja nus hons pris ne dira sa raison*
> *adroitement, se dolantement non;*
> *mes par confort puet il fere chançon.*
> *moult ai amis, mes povre sont li don;*
> *honte en avront, se por mes reançon*
> *sui ces deus yvers pris.*
>
> *Ce servent bien mi homme et mi baron,*
> *Englois, Normant, Poitevin et Gascon,*
> *que je n'avoir si povre conpaignon,*
> *cui je laissasse por avoir en prixon.*
> *je nel di pas por nule retraçon,*
> *mes encor sui ge pris.*
>
> No prisoner pleads well his case,
> Framing it sorrowfully. But,
> To comfort his distress, he can make a song.
> My friends are many, though their gifts are few.
> Shame upon them, if my ransom is not paid
> These two winters in prison.
>
> My friends and barons know well -
> English, Norman, Poitevin and Gascon all -
> That no friend of mine so low
> Would I leave in prison for want of cash.
> I mean no reproach
> But still am I held captive.
>
> (*Richard Coeur de Lion* trans: Caitlín Matthews)

The Romance of Richard Coeur de Lion

The following three extracts are from a redaction of a fourteenth century English romance based on an earlier French work. It contains a strange mixture of history and fantastic invention: the account of the Crusade being more or less accurate, but with the addition of episodes of imaginary adventures demonstrating the way in which Richard had become a larger-than-life figure of truly mythic proportions. They tell the curious story of Richard's birth, and of his single combat with Saladin. They are taken from George Ellis' *Specimens of Early English Metrical Romances* of 1848, further edited by the present author. They give a startling portrait of Richard, very far from that of history, but very much in the manner of the time and of the legendary quality possessed by the King.

The Birth of a Hero
Lord, King of Glory, what favours didst thou bestow on King Richard! How edifying is it to read the history of his conquests! Many acts of

chivalry are familiarly known; the deeds of Charlemagne and Turpin, and of their knights Ogier le Danois, Roland, and Oliver; those of Alexander; those of Arthur and Gawain; and even the ancient wars of Troy and the exploits of Hector and Achilles, are already current in rhyme. But the glory of Richard and of the peerless knights of England, his companions, is at present exhibited only in French books, which not more than one in a hundred of unlearned men can understand. This story, lordings, I propose to tell you; and may the blessing of God be on those who will listen to me with attention!

The father of Richard was King Henry; in whose reign, as I find in my original, Saint Thomas was slain at the altar of the cathedral of Canterbury, where miracles are wrought to this day. King Henry, when twenty years of age, was a prince of great valour; but having a dislike to matrimony, could not be induced to take a wife on account of her wealth or power; and only acceded to the entreaties of his barons, on the condition of their providing for his consort the most beautiful woman in the universe.

Ambassadors were immediately dispatched in every direction to search for this paragon. One party of them was carried, by a fair wind, into the midst of the ocean, where they were suddenly arrested by a calm which threatened to prevent the further prosecution of their voyage. Fortunately, the breeze had already brought them nearly in contact with another vessel, which by its astonishing magnificence engrossed their whole attention. Every nail seemed to be headed with gold; the deck was painted with azure and inlaid with ivory; the rudder appeared to be of pure gold; the mast was of ivory; the sails of satin; the ropes of silk; an awning of cloth of gold was spread above the deck; and under this awning were assembled divers knights and ladies most superbly dressed, appearing to form the court of a princess whose beauty was bright as the sun through the glass. Our ambassadors were hailed by this splendid company, and questioned about the object of their voyage: which being explained, they were conducted on board, and received with proper ceremony by the stranger king, who rose from his chair, composed of a single carbuncle stone, to salute them. Trestles were immediately set; a table covered with a silken cloth was laid; a rich repast, ushered in by the sound of trumpets and shalms, was served up; and the English knights had full leisure during dinner to contemplate the charms of the incomparable princess, who was seated near her father. The king then informed them that he had been instructed by a vision to set sail for England with his daughter; and the ambassadors, delighted at finding the success of their search confirmed with this preternatural authority, proposed to accompany him without loss of time to their master. A north-easterly wind springing up at the moment, they set sail, entered the Thames, and soon cast anchor off the Tower; where King Henry happened to be lodged, and was informed by his ambassadors of their safe arrival.

A Knight Templar, the most feared order of knighthood in the Holy Land. They were monks as well as warriors, dedicated to a spiritual life and to the recapture of the holy places in Jerusalem. They guided and protected pilgrims during the Middle Ages.

Henry made immediate preparations for the reception of the royal visitors. Attended by his whole court, he went to meet and welcome them at the water-side; from whence the whole company, preceded by bands of minstrels, marched in procession to the royal palace at Westminster, the streets through which they passed being hung with cloth of gold. A magnificent entertainment was provided; after which Henry having thus fulfilled the duties of hospitality addressed the stranger king:

> *'Lief Sire, what is thy name?'*
> *'My name,' he said, 'is Corbaring;*
> *Of Antioch I am king.'*
> *And told him, in his resoun* [oration]*,*
> *He came thither thorough a vision.*
> *'For sothe, Sire, I telle thee,*
> *I had else brought more meynie;*
> *Many mo, withouten fail,*
> *And mo shippes with vitail.'*
> *Then asked he that lady bright,*
> *'What hightest thou, my sweet wight?'*
> *'Cassodorien, withouten leasing.'*
> *Thus answered she the king.*
> *'Damsel,' he said, 'bright and sheen,*
> *Wilt thou dwell and be my queen?'*
> *She answered, with words still,*
> *'Sire, I am at my father's will.'*

After this courtship the king of Antioch, who was no friend to unnecessary delays, proposed that they should be betrothed on that night; and that the nuptials, which he wished to be private, should be celebrated on the following morning.

These conditions were readily accepted, and the fair Cassodorien received the nuptial benediction; but the ceremony was attended with an untoward accident. At the elevation of the host, the young queen fainted away; and her swoon continued so long that it became necessary to carry her out of church into an adjoining chamber. The spectators were much alarmed at this unlucky omen; and she was herself so disturbed by it, that she made a vow never more to assist at any of the sacraments: but it does not seem to have much interrupted the happiness of the royal couple, because the queen became successively the mother of three children; Richard, John, and a daughter named Topyas.

During fifteen years, Cassodorien was permitted to persevere in her resolution without any remonstrance from King Henry; but unluckily, after this period, one of his principal barons remarked to him that her conduct gave general scandal, and requested his permission to detain her in church from the commencement of the mass till its termination. Henry consented; and when the queen, on hearing the bell which announced the celebration of the sacrament, prepared to leave the church, the baron opposed her departure, and attempted to detain her by force. The event of the experiment was extraordinary. Cassodorien,

seizing her daughter with one hand, and Prince John with the other,

Out of the roof she gan her dight [prepared to depart]
Openly, before all their sight!
John fell from the air, in that stound,
And brake his thigh on the ground;
And with her daughter she fled away,
That never after she was y-seye [seen].

Henry repented, when it was too late, of his deference to the advice of his courtiers. Inconsolable for the loss of the beautiful Cassodorien, he languished for a short time, and then died, leaving his dominions to his eldest son Richard, who was now in his fifteenth year, and was already distinguished by his premature excellence in all the exercises of chivalry.

Battle at Sea
Richard now prepared for his grand expedition, and, having confided

A battle at sea between crusaders and Saracens. On his way to the Holy Land, Richard met with one of the ships running the blockade around Acre. He defeated the Moslem sailors with consummate ease.

39

the government of Cyprus to the Earl of Leicester, set sail for Syria with a fleet of two hundred transports under convoy of fifteen well-armed galleys. For the first ten days the weather was perfectly favourable; but on the eleventh they met with a violent storm, during which it was difficult to prevent the dispersion of the armament. At length the sky cleared, and they discovered in the offing a *dromound,* or ship of burthen of vast size, and laden nearly to the water's edge. Alain Trenchemer was dispatched, in a light vessel, to inquire whither she was bound, whose property she was, and what was her cargo and was answered by a *latimer* (an interpreter) that she came from Apulia, was laden with provisions for the use of the French army, and was bound to Acres. But Alain, perceiving only one man on deck who answered his questions, insisted on seeing the rest of the crew, whom he suspected to be Saracens; and after a few evasions on the part of the latimer, the whole ship's company suddenly came upon deck, and answered him by a general shout of defiance. Alain hastily returned with this report to the king; who, arming himself with all expedition, threw himself into a galley, and ordered his rowers to make every possible exertion.

> 'Roweth on fast! Who that is faint,
> In evil water may he be dreynt!'
> They rowed hard, and sung thereto
> With hevelow and rumbeloo.

Richard's impatience being thus seconded by the zeal of his men, the galley flew like an arrow from a cross-bow; and Alain steered the vessel with such skill, that, encountering the stern of the dromound, it cut off a considerable part of her quarter. The king made every effort to board; but the deck was covered with well-armed Saracens; and others from the 'top castles' assaulted the galley with such showers of heavy stones, that Richard was in the most imminent danger. At length, seven more galleys being detached to his assistance, and the enemies attacked in every direction, he sprang on board of the dromound, and, setting his back against the mast, clove many of the Saracens to the middle, cut off the heads of others, and amputated arms and legs in every direction; till the unbelievers, who at first consisted of sixteen hundred men, were reduced to thirty.

A Fatal Combat
It was now determined to attempt, without further delay, the siege of Nineveh; but intelligence being received that the Saracens were assembling in great numbers in the plain of Odoh, it became necessary to defeat them in the first instance. Richard, dividing the Christians into four parts, directed them to take different routes, so as to arrive on the field and make their attack on four opposite points: he also ordered them to display only the Saracen standards which they had captured in the field of Arsour. By this strategem the enemy were completely surprised and

routed, excepting a small body, which, not being pressed with sufficient vigour by Philip's division, retreated in good order to Nineveh.

The siege of that city was next undertaken; and the military engines being brought up to the walls, the mangonels began to cast stones, and at the same time

> *Arrowblast of vys, with quarrell,*
> *With staff-slings that smite well,*
> *With trepegettes they slungen also;*
> *That wrought hem full mickle wo!*
> *And blew wild fire in trumpes of gin*
> *To mickle sorrow to hem within.*

But these tardy operations were soon suspended by a proposal from the garrison, to which King Richard most joyfully consented; viz., that the fate of the place and of its dependencies should be decided by a combat between three Saracen and three Christian champions. Sir Archolyn, Sir Coudyrbras, and Sir Calabre were respectively opposed to Richard, Sir Thomas Tourneham, and Sir Fulk Doyley, and had the honour of contesting, for a short time, the victory with the three bravest knights in the world. The issue of the combat, however, proved fatal to the Mahometan champions; the city was surrendered; and the garrison and inhabitants, who had been spectators of the battle, being convinced that the best religion was that which conferred military superiority, came in crowds to be baptized, and to follow the standard of the conquerors.

Saladin, in the mean time, had retreated to Babylon, where he again assembled a vast army; but, being surprised by the sudden march of his enemies, was unexpectedly besieged by them in his capital. The Christians, well aware of the advantage of attacking him in a position where his cavalry was perfectly useless, lost no time in completing the blockade.

Richard, always indefatigable, harassed the besieged by constant night attacks, in which the flights of quarrells and arrows from his engines did great execution; and, during the day, employed his mangonels to beat down the outworks and approaches to the city. In short, the romancer assures us that the destruction of Saladin and his whole army would have been unavoidable, had not Philip been bribed by the vast treasures sent by the besieged to withdraw his forces, under pretence of wanting provisions, and thus to prevent the continuation of the blockade.

Saladin, being thus enabled to meet his enemy once more in the field, sent a messenger to offer battle; and at the same time a challenge to King Richard, to meet him in single combat in front of the two armies, for the purpose of deciding their respective pretensions, and of ascertaining whether 'Jesus or Jupiter' was the more powerful divinity. The challenge was accompanied by the offer of a war-horse, far superior in strength and activity to Favel of Cyprus or Lyard of Prys (the favourite horses of Richard), which it was proposed that he should ride on the occasion.

It seems that a necromancer, a 'noble clerk', had conjured two 'strong

A Knight Hospitaller. Together with the Templars, they were the greatest and most feared soldiers in the Holy Land.

fiends of the air' into the likeness of a mare and her colt; and that the younger devil had received instructions to kneel down and suck his dam as often as she, by neighing, should give him a signal for the purpose. Such an attitude could not but prove very inconvenient to his rider, who would thus be nearly at the mercy of his antagonist; and it was hoped that Saladin, being mounted on the mare, would obtain an easy victory. Richard, ignorant of this conspiracy against his life and honour, readily accepted all the conditions; the horse was sent on the morning of the battle to the Christian camp; and the hopes of the fiend and of the Sultan seemed on the point of being realized.

But, during the preceding night, an angel had appeared to the Christian hero; had related the machinations of the Saracens; had given him full instructions for the management of his diabolical steed; and had presented to him a spearhead, which no armour, however enchanted, was able to resist. At the first dawn of day the hostile armies began to form in order of battle. That of the Saracens, occupying an extent of ten miles in front, threatened to surround the inferior forces of the Christians;

> As snow ligges on the mountains,
> Be-helied [covered over] were hills and plains,
> With hauberk bright and helmes clear.
> Of trumpes and of tabourer
> To hear the noise it was wonder:
> As though the earth above and under
> Should fallen, so fared the sound!

Richard, however, perfectly indifferent about the numbers of the infidels, pointed them out to his troops as a multitude of victims whom heaven had destined to sacrifice; and, calling for his arms and horse, immediately prepared for battle.

The fiend horse being led forth, the king, in conformity to the angel's instructions, conjured him, in the name of the Trinity, to submit to his guidance in the battle; and the fiend having shaken his head in token of acquiescence, he ordered that the creature's ears should be closely stopped with wax, and that he should be caparisoned in the manner prescribed by the messenger of Heaven.

The reins of his bridle, the crupper, the girths, and the peytrel [breast plate] were of steel chain; the saddle-bows were of iron, and supported two hooks, by which was fixed a ponderous beam of wood, forty feet in length, lying across the horse's mane, and intended to bear down, at every evolution of the animal, whatever body of enemies might attempt to oppose his progress. From the lower part of the saddle-bows were suspended on one side the formidable battle-axe, always so fatal to the Saracens, and on the other a brazen club. The king, arrayed in splints of steel, which were again covered by a complete coat of mail; his helmet surmounted by the dove perching on a cross, the symbol of the Holy Ghost; his shield, emblazoned with three leopards, on his shoulder; and bearing in his hand the spear, on whose point was engraven the holy name of God, only waited till the terms of the battle between himself and Saladin should be publicly read, and assented to by both parties; and then, springing into the saddle, set spurs to his steed, and flew with the rapidity of lightning to the encounter.

Saladin, throwing his shield before him, rushed to the charge with equal impetuosity; but as he trusted principally to his mare, he was unwilling to encumber himself with a spear, and only bore in his hand a broad scymitar, with which he proposed to cut off the head of his prostrate enemy. The mare, indeed, exerted herself to the utmost: she shook with violence the numberless bells with which her bridle and housings were completely covered, and neighed with all her might; but the colt-fiend, whose ears were closely stopped, was insensible to a noise, which almost deafened both armies. Far from relaxing, he seemed to increase his speed, and met his unfortunate dam with a shock which she was not all prepared to resist.

Her girth and bridle instantly burst; she rolled on the plain: at the same time the spear of Richard passed through the serpent painted on the sultan's shield, penetrated his armour and part of the shoulder, and threw him, with his heels in the air, to a distance on the plain. Richard, without further troubling himself about the sultan or his mare, rode at full speed into the midst of the Saracen phalanx; overset with his beam twenty unbelievers on each side of his saddle; and, whirling his battle-axe, beheaded or clove to the chine every enemy within his reach. The earl of Salisbury, Doyley, Tourneham, and his other brave knights closely followed, and assisted in dissipating such of the enemy as ventured to resist; and Philip, with his Frenchmen, valiantly assailed the fugitives.

The rout soon became general:

> To tell the sooth in all things,
> In the Gest as we find,
> That mo than sixty thousand
> Of empty steeds abouten yode
> Up to the fetlocks in blood.

In the mean time, the citizens of Babylon, seeing from their walls the defeat of their countrymen, opened their gates to the victors; and Saladin, when recovered from his fall, seeing that all was lost, set spurs to his mare, and escaped into a thick wood, where Richard, encumbered by his beam, was unable to follow him.

Of the inhabitants of Babylon, the greater number consented to be baptized: those who refused were, as usual, put to the sword; and the riches found in the town were distributed among the conquerors, who, after a fortnight spent in feasts and rejoicing, proceeded on their march towards Jerusalem, the reduction of which seemed to promise no considerable difficulty.

★   ★   ★

Tho afterward, all the three year,
Christian men, both far and near,
Yeden the way to Jerusalem,
To the sepulchre, and to Bethlem,
To Olivet, and to Nazarel,
And to Imaus castel,
And to all other pilgrimage,
Withouten harm or damage.
King Richard, doughty of hand,
Turned homeward to England.
King Richard reigned here
No more but ten year.
Sithen, he was shot, alas!
In castel Gaillard there he was.
Thus ended Richard our King:
God give us all good ending!
And his soul rest and roo [repose],
And our souls, when we come thereto!
    Amen. Explicit.

The Abbey of Fontrevault in the Loire valley, founded in the twelfth century by Benedictine nuns, became the burial place of many of the Plantagenets. The magnificent tombs contain the remains of Henry II, Eleanor of Aquitaine, Isabella of Angouleme (wife of John) and the Lionheart himself, whose tomb effigy is shown here.

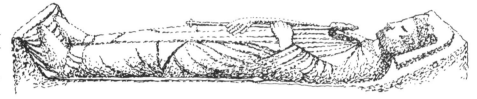

GENEALOGY OF CHARACTERS

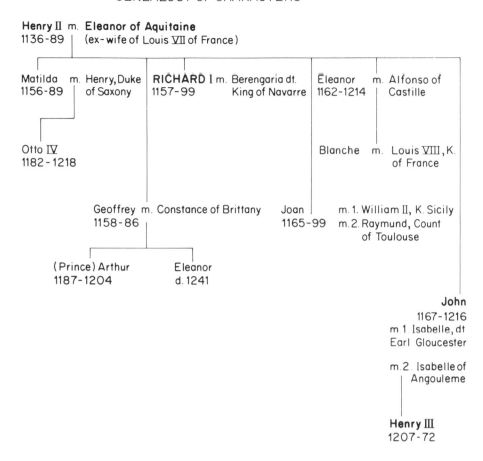

Henry II m. **Eleanor of Aquitaine**
1136-89 | (ex-wife of Louis VII of France)

Matilda m. Henry, Duke
1156-89 | of Saxony

RICHARD I m. Berengaria dt.
1157-99 | King of Navarre

Eleanor m. Alfonso of
1162-1214 | Castille

Otto IV
1182-1218

Blanche m. Louis VIII, K.
of France

Geoffrey m. Constance of Brittany
1158-86 |

Joan m. 1. William II, K. Sicily
1165-99 | m. 2. Raymund, Count
of Toulouse

(Prince) Arthur
1187-1204

Eleanor
d. 1241

John
1167-1216
m 1. Isabelle, dt
Earl Gloucester

m. 2. Isabelle of
Angouleme

Henry III
1207-72

Bibliography

Barber, R. *The Devil's Crown* BBC, 1978
Barber, R. *The Reign of Chivalry* David and Charles, 1980
Billings, M. *The Cross and the Crescent* BBC, 1987.
Bridge, A. *The Crusades* Granada, 1980
Duggan, A. *The Devil's Brood* Faber & Faber, 1957
Foss, M. *Chivalry* Book Club Associates, 1975
Fossier, R. (ed.) *Cambridge Illustrated History of the Middle Ages 1250–1520* Cambridge University Press, 1986
Gillingham, J. *The Life & Times of Richard I* Weidenfeld & Nicolson, 1973
Hallam, E. (ed.) *The Plantagenet Chronicles* Weidenfeld & Nicolson, 1986
Hampden, J. (ed.) *Crusader King* Ward, 1956
Henderson, P. *Richard Coeur de Lion* Hale, 1958

Holbach, M.M. *In the Footsteps of Richard Coeur de Lion* Stanley Paul, 1912
Keen, M. *Chivalry* Yale University Press, 1984
Koch, H.W. *Medieval Warfare* Bison Books, 1978
Koenigsburger, H.G. *Medieval Europe* Longmans, 1987
Newark, T. *Medieval Warfare* Jupiter Books, 1979
Newark, T. *Medieval Warlords* Blandford Press, 1987
Norgate, K. *Richard the Lion Heart* Longman, 1924
Runicman, S. *A History of the Crusades* Cambridge University Press, 1951–4
Tarassuk, L. and Blair, C. (ed.) *The Complete Encyclopedia of Arms and Weapons* Batsford, 1979
Turnbull, S. *The World of the Medieval Knight* Arms & Armour Press, 1986

FRANCE

Trifels■

BOHEMIA

MORAVIA

• Vézelay

AUSTRIA
Durnstein■ •Vienna

BAVARIA

HUNGARY

HOLY ROMAN EMPIRE

THE ALPS

• Lyons

KINGDOM OF ITALY
Genoa

Belgrade•

• Nice

TUSCANY

Marseilles

ADRIATIC SEA

CORSICA

Rome•

KINGDOM
OF SICILY

Naples•
•Salerno

BYZANTINE

SARDINIA

MEDITERRANEAN SEA

Messina

SICILY

—--—--— Boundary of the Holy Roman Empire

——————▶ Richard's route

—·—·—▶ Richard's journey before his arrest by Leopold

··········▶ Route of Barbarossa's army 1190

— — — ▶ Philip Augustus' route

■ Castles where Richard was imprisoned

▨ Patrimony of St Peter

0   100   200   300 miles

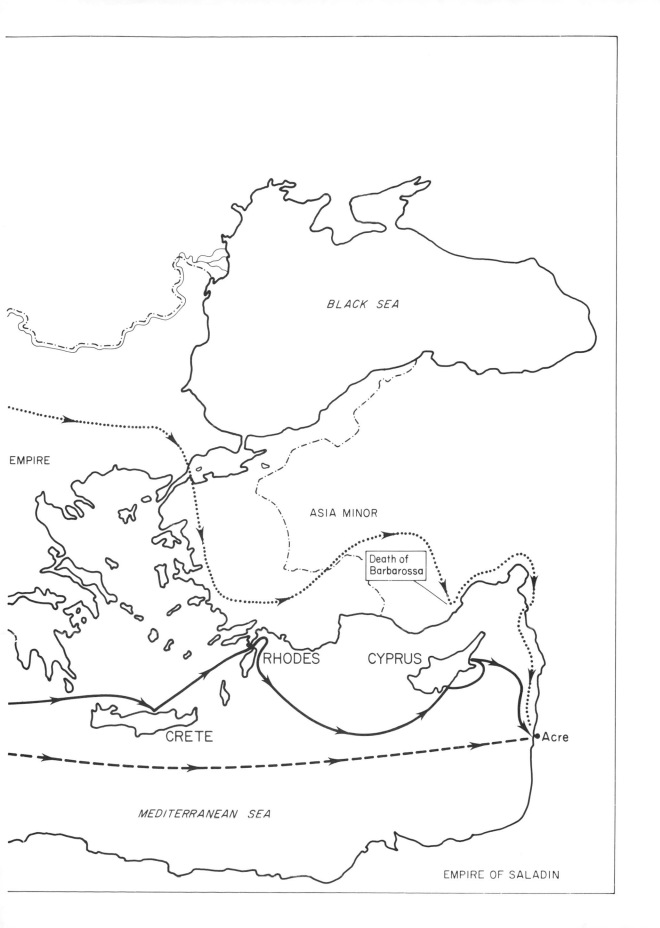

BLACK SEA

EMPIRE

ASIA MINOR

Death of
Barbarossa

RHODES

CYPRUS

CRETE

Acre

MEDITERRANEAN SEA

EMPIRE OF SALADIN

Index

Page numbers in *italics* refer to illustrations.

Illustrations

Colour plates by James Field.
Line illustrations by Chesca Potter.
Maps and diagrams by Chartwell Illustrators.
Photographs courtesy of: Bildarchiv Foto Marburg (page 29); Department of the Environment and Crown Copyright (page 35); French Government Tourist Office (pages 31 and 44); Cyprus Tourist Board (page 17); Peter Newark's Historical Pictures (pages 8, 11, 15, 22, 25, 32, 33, 34 and 39).